THE
POWHATAN
INDIANS

THE JUNIOR LIBRARY OF AMERICAN INDIANS

THE POWHATAN INDIANS

Melissa McDaniel

CHELSEA JUNIORS

a division of CHELSEA HOUSE PUBLISHERS

FRONTISPIECE: A watercolor of a *werowance* painted by John White in 1585.

CHAPTER TITLE ORNAMENT: A drawing of the Powhatan god Okewas.

English-language words that are italicized in the text can be found in the glossary at the back of the book.

Chelsea House Publishers
EDITORIAL DIRECTOR Richard Rennert
EXECUTIVE MANAGING EDITOR Karyn Gullen Browne
COPY CHIEF Robin James
PICTURE EDITOR Adrian G. Allen
CREATIVE DIRECTOR Robert Mitchell
ART DIRECTOR Joan Ferrigno
PRODUCTION MANAGER Sallye Scott

The Junior Library of American Indians
SENIOR EDITOR Martin Schwabacher

Staff for THE POWHATAN INDIANS
EDITORIAL ASSISTANT Erin McKenna
ASSISTANT DESIGNER Lydia Rivera
PICTURE RESEARCHER Sandy Jones
COVER ILLUSTRATOR Hal Just

3 5 7 9 8 6 4 2

Library of Congress Cataloging-in-Publication Data

McDaniel, Melissa.
The Powhatan Indians / Melissa McDaniel.
  p. cm.— (The Junior Library of American Indians)
Includes index.
        0-7910-2494-6
        0-7910-2495-4 (pbk.)
1. Powhatan Indians—History—Juvenile Literature. 2. Powhatan Indi-ans—Social Life and Customs—Juvenile Literature. I. Title. II. Series.
E99.P85M33 1995   95-2497
975'.004973—dc20   CIP
                                                          AC

CONTENTS

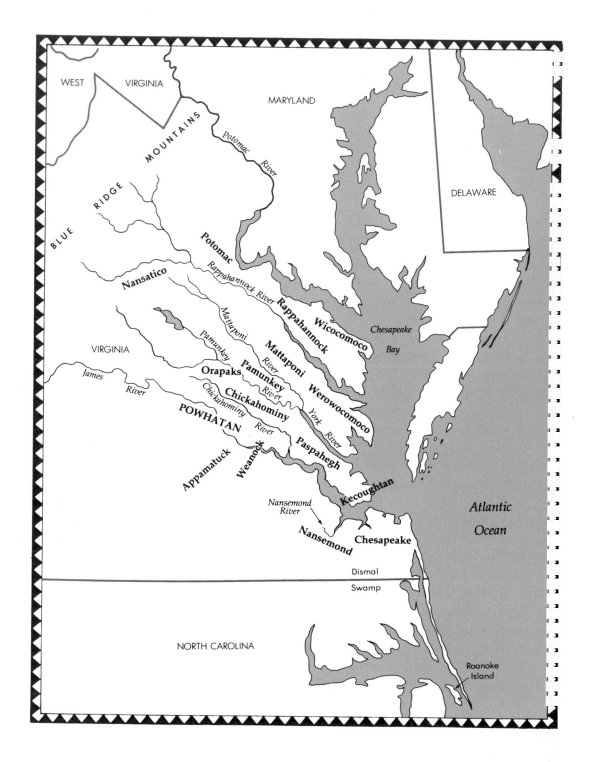

A map showing the locations of the Tidewater tribes of Virginia.

Chapter **1**

Two Legends

In the beginning of time, the Hare created human beings. At first, he kept his new creations in a giant bag in his house. One day, the winds from the four directions visited the Hare's home. They discovered the men and women the Hare had made and wanted to eat them. The Hare scolded the wind for making such a suggestion and sent them away.

The Hare then created water, land, and one great deer to feed upon the land. Still angry at the Hare, the four winds returned, killed the deer, ate it, and left again. The Hare took the hairs from the dead deer's body and spread them out over the earth. Speaking powerful words, he changed each hair into a deer. He then opened his bag of humans and put one man and one woman in each country, creating the beginning of mankind.

This is how a Potomac Indian who lived 400 years ago described the creation of the world. The Potomacs were one of about 30 Indian groups who lived along the Atlantic Ocean near Chesapeake Bay in the present-day states of Virginia and Maryland. These tribes had very similar languages and cultures. Near the end of the 16th century, many of them fell under the rule of Powhatan, the leader of one group. Because Powhatan created an empire that included most of the Indian villages in the area, together they are called the Powhatan tribes.

Although he lent his name to a kingdom containing thousands of people, Powhatan is not the most famous member of the Powhatan tribes. That honor belongs to his daughter Pocahontas, the prime figure in one of the most celebrated stories in American history. The story goes back to the very beginning of the English *colonial* efforts in America.

In 1607, British colonists founded Jamestown, the first permanent English settlement in North America. Jamestown was located on the James River in what is now Virginia, right in the heart of Powhatan's

An oil painting of Pocahontas dressed as an English noblewoman. Pocahontas, the daughter of Powhatan, married an Englishman and met the queen of England.

territory. While exploring the surrounding area, one of the settlement's leaders, Captain John Smith, was captured by Native Americans. According to Smith, he was taken to Powhatan's village and forced to kneel on a stone altar. Just when an Indian warrior was about to smash his skull with a heavy club, Pocahontas, who was then about 12 years old, flung herself over his body, protecting him from harm. She pleaded with her father to spare Smith's life. Powhatan, who adored his young daughter, relented, allowing Smith to leave unscathed.

As legend has it, Pocahontas also helped the starving colonists by convincing her fellow tribespeople to provide them with food. This food enabled the Jamestown colony to survive the harsh early months of 1608. Because of her generosity, Pocahontas is said to have rescued not only Smith but the entire colony. And because Jamestown survived, she made possible the development of the United States of America.

For centuries, the story of Pocahontas's rescue of John Smith was believed to be true. But now many historians think it is inaccurate. Some believe that Smith was actually experiencing a ritualized adoption ceremony making him a member of Powhatan's tribe. Others believe that the event never happened at all because Smith did not mention Pocahontas in print until 1624, the third time he wrote about his captivity by the Indians. In Smith's earlier accounts, he wrote that Powhatan had treated him kindly and released him.

Though the legend of Pocahontas is well known, the story of her father, her people, and their relations with the first British settlers in North America has been told much less often. Yet the history of the Tidewater Indians, both before and after the arrival of the Europeans, is as full of drama and conflict as the legends surrounding Pocahontas.

Four centuries after their first contact with the English colonists, members of these proud tribes are still living in the state of Virginia. There they continue to keep alive the complex and fascinating society they created long before white people ever set foot in America. ▲

An engraving by Theodore de Bry, published in 1590, shows Tidewater Indians making a canoe by burning and scraping out the inside of a log.

Chapter 2

Life in the Tidewater

The Powhatan tribes lived in the part of Virginia known as the Tidewater. This region earned its name because the many rivers flowing through the coastal lowlands into Chesapeake Bay are affected by the tides. Their water is a mixture of fresh water and salt water from the ocean.

When the English first arrived, there were at least 14,000 Powhatans living in many small villages in the area. These towns were usually built on high ground along rivers so that the Indians could see others approaching. Where the river water was salty, the Indians made sure their towns were near

freshwater springs so they could obtain drinking water. Powhatan towns rarely contained more than 20 houses, which were scattered in groups separated by fields, rather than lined up in rows along streets.

Powhatan houses were shaped like tunnels. They were built by sticking two rows of *saplings* into the ground, bending them over, and tying them together at the top. Poles were tied across the bent saplings to form

A modern replica of a Powhatan home in Jamestown Festival Park, Virginia.

a framework. To make walls and a roof, the framework was covered with mats woven from marsh reeds or bark. Each house consisted of one large room with an entrance at each end. A fire was kept burning in the middle of the house at all times. The smoke escaped through a hole in the roof. If the house was too dark or smoky, some of the mats were rolled up like window blinds, allowing fresh air to flow freely through the house.

Building and maintaining houses was the responsibility of women. They also wove mats and baskets, *tanned* animal hides to make clothing and bags, and made pots, utensils, and tools. Their chief task, however, was farming.

Each spring, Powhatan women, with the help of children and some elderly men, planted corn, beans, squash, and passion-flowers in the nearby fields. They put a few kernels of corn and some beans together in mounds of dirt. Other vegetables were planted in between the mounds. One plant, however, was grown apart from the others—tobacco. Tobacco was important in Powhatan religious and political rituals, but it was completely unknown to Europeans before they arrived in the Americas.

The Powhatans planted four types of corn, which ripened at different times. That way, fresh corn was available from early June until October. They would either roast the corn in a fire or grind it up, wrap it in cornhusks, and boil it. They also sucked out the juice from the cornstalks, which was delightfully sweet. Some of the corn was saved to be used as seed the following year. The Powhatans also dried some corn to use during winter by laying it on thick mats in the sun. After it was dried, corn could be boiled for eating or pounded into cornmeal. Cornmeal was used to thicken stews and to make bread. In the summer, women gathered wild strawberries, raspberries, apples, and grapes in the forests. They also dug up wild potatoes. In the fall, they collected walnuts, hickory nuts, chestnuts, and acorns. These nuts were eaten raw or dried for future use. They could also be boiled to make delicacies like "walnut milk," a pudding made from ground-up hickory nuts and water. On special occasions, squash was added to walnut milk. The nuts collected by the women also provided the tribes with valuable oils that were used in cooking and as medicines.

While the women were tending the fields and gathering, and drying food, the men

An engraving by Theodore de Bry showing Powhatan Indians drying fish to store for the winter.

were hunting and fishing. Canoes were vital to the Powhatans' success as fishermen. Each canoe was made from a single log. The log was hollowed out by using stone axes or by burning sections and then scraping away the soft, charred wood. Some of these canoes were 50 feet long and could hold 40 people, along with their paddles, fishing gear, and temporary shelters.

The Powhatans used many methods to catch fish, both from land and from canoes. Sometimes they used rods with hooks made of bone. They also used nets made from deer *sinew*, tree bark, or rope that the women had spun by hand from plant fibers. Fishermen shot fish with arrows tied to cords and speared fish that were in shallow water. They also made traps called weirs by placing stones across the river in the shape of a V. When the fish swam into the point of the V, they were caught in a large wicker trap.

Fish were either roasted on a frame over a fire or boiled in a stew. They could be smoked and dried by moving the cooking frame farther from the fire. Smoked fish often lasted more than a month before going bad.

Although fishing provided the Powhatans with a regular source of food, men took more pride in hunting, which supplied not only food but also skins for clothing. Hunting required great skill in the dense, dark woods of the Tidewater. Men often hunted alone, using a wooden bow with a string made of twisted deerskin or animal gut. Their arrows had points made of bird beaks, bones, antlers, or stones. Sometimes hunters disguised themselves as deer in order to get closer to their prey. After stuffing the head of a deerskin, a hunter would drape the rest of the skin over his arm. If a deer looked up when a hunter approached, the hunter would move the dead deer's head to mimic a live deer. Seeing another deer, the prey remained calm, rather than fleeing as it would at the sight of a human. This enabled the hunter to take careful aim.

Another hunting method required many men working together. When hunters encountered a herd of deer, they would form a large circle around it. Then they built fires and began shouting. The deer would dart between the fires, trying to run away, only to find the hunters there ready to shoot them. By surrounding a herd, a group of hunters could kill up to 15 deer at a time. If a herd was on a point of land jutting into the water, a similar method was used. Some of the men cut off the deer's escape route, forcing the deer into the water, where hunters in canoes were waiting for them.

The Powhatans also hunted muskrats, rabbits, squirrels, raccoons, opossums, and wild turkeys, and they trapped beavers and otters. Bear was valued both as a gourmet delicacy and for the oil from its fat, which was used to make paint for their bodies.

Hunting provided the skins that the Powhatans used for clothing. But because of the warm climate, they often wore very little. Young girls wore no clothes at all until they reached *puberty*. Both men and women usually wore nothing but *loincloths* made from deerskin or grass. For hunting or war expeditions, deerskin leggings and moccasins were added to the costume. Wealthier people wore leather robes embroidered with shells and beads.

Even in winter, the Powhatans went as long as possible without wearing extra layers of clothing. They preferred to simply adjust to the cold. Children were prepared for this right from the start. After a baby was born, it was dipped in water, regardless of how cold the season. Throughout their early years, children were washed every day, and their skin was oiled and painted to make it better able to withstand the cold. Sometimes adults also oiled their bodies to help keep themselves warm. When they could endure the cold no longer, they donned fur cloaks. In winter, the rich wore warm, shiny robes made from woven feathers.

Throughout the summer months when food was plentiful, the Powhatans spent most evenings making music, dancing, and playing games. The Powhatans played deerskin drums, flutes fashioned from cane, and rattles made from dried gourds. They also wrestled, held footraces, and had contests to see who could kick a ball the farthest. Men played a game similar to field hockey, in which they used sticks to hit a leather ball between two trees that served as the goal. Women and boys played a game similar to soccer.

As the weather grew colder, the tribes prepared for their annual winter hunt. They stored dried food on mat-covered *scaffolds* next to their houses or in holes they dug in the woods. Everyone except the very old and the very young moved west, where there were more deer. Women carried the household items and rolled-up mats to make new houses, leaving the men free to be on constant alert for game or enemies. Men spent the winter days hunting, while women set up temporary camps, cooked, and tanned skins.

In early spring, the Powhatans gathered their belongings and returned to their permanent villages, and the cycle of planting and hunting began again. By adapting and adjusting to the changing seasons, they enjoyed a varied way of life that satisfied all their physical needs. ▲

*An engraving of the god
Okewas, whom the
Powhatans considered
so powerful that they
carried images of him
into battle.*

Chapter 3

Powhatan Society

The Powhatan tribes had a complex society consisting of many different ranks. There were priests, councillors, and ruling families who were much wealthier than ordinary people.

Each tribe was ruled by a leader called a *werowance* or, if a woman, a *weronsqua*. These positions were passed down through families. But rather than passing the title from father to son, the Powhatans used a type of matrilineal succession, meaning the title was passed through women. The order of succession went from the werowance's mother's oldest son to the youngest, then from her oldest daughter to the youngest. When there were no more living children, the title passed to her oldest daughter's firstborn son. Thus women could be leaders, but only if they had no surviving brothers.

Werowances had great wealth, most of it obtained through *tribute* paid by the common people. Tribute given to werowances included skins, corn, game, and copper. This wealth enabled them to have sumptuous lifestyles. They ate lavish meals and wore warm, elaborately decorated robes. Their houses were much larger than those of ordinary people; some were 40 yards long. A werowance's house had an entrance only at one end. A visitor had to walk through long, dark passageways before coming to the chamber where the ruler greeted guests.

Accompanying this great wealth was near absolute power, including life-and-death power over their subjects. Minor offenses could bring swift beatings with a club, while more serious offenses, such as murder, theft from a fellow tribesmember, or disobeying the werowance, were punishable by death. In one case in 1676, a werowance was negotiating with the English. While he was speaking, one of his subjects interrupted him. The werowance raised his tomahawk and split the rude man's head open. He then continued the conversation as if nothing had happened. Most of the time, however, punishments were carried out by an assistant.

The next most prominent members of Powhatan society were *quiyoughcosucks*, or priests. Because it was believed that priests could foretell the future, including whether raids would be successful, they were valued advisers to the werowances. Priests were thought to be able to control the weather and confuse enemies during warfare. They also served as the tribal doctors, using medicinal plants and roots to cure the sick.

Perhaps their most important function was their ability to summon and converse with Okewas, the most powerful god in the Powhatan religion. Okewas was a harsh and *vengeful* spirit whose language only the priests could understand. Sometimes he would appear in the woods in the form of a handsome young man. The Powhatans believed that any trouble they faced, such as illnesses or bad harvests, was a punishment from Okewas. To appease him, they gave him offerings of tobacco, shells, and copper. Okewas was considered so powerful that warriors carried his image into battle.

Images of Okewas were also housed in village temples. Temples were about 100 feet long and aligned in an east-west direction, with a door only on the east end. The first of the many rooms contained a fire that the priests kept lit continuously. The most westerly room contained the bodies of dead werowances and wooden images of Oke-was and other gods. These temples also served as storehouses for the rulers' wealth. Skins, corn, and jewelry were all kept here, guarded by the gods.

Besides the tribal werowances, each village had its own werowance who paid tribute to those above him and received tribute from those beneath him. Below village werowances in rank were councillors, men who gained prestige and wealth through their exploits in hunting or warfare and who advised rulers. Along with priests and werowances, these men comprised the council that declared war.

The Powhatans waged war for revenge, to gain territory, and to *abduct* women and children. Although men who were captured during warfare were usually tortured and killed, women, children, and rulers were often adopted into the tribe.

The Powhatans wore elaborate jewelry and other decorations, which often indicated a person's status in society. Beads made from shells were commonly used to make earrings, necklaces, headbands, and embroidery for clothing. Copper was more rare and was worn solely by the rich. Only certain

A 1586 watercolor by John White of a tribal priest, or quiyoughcosuck. The small lock of hair behind his ear showed his rank.

chiefs were allowed to wear headbands made of copper.

Both men and women usually had their ears pierced two or three times, but the fancier and more flamboyant earrings were reserved for men. In addition to beads, men wore earrings made of birds' feet and bear and cougar claws, which were sometimes decorated with copper. John Smith reported seeing a man wearing as an earring "a small greene and yellow coloured snake, neare halfe a yard in length, which crawling and lapping her selfe about his necke oftentimes familiarly would kisse his lips. Others weare a dead Rat tyed by the taile."

While men had the more elaborate earrings, only women wore tattoos. To make tattoos, they slit their skin with a heated knife and rubbed soot into the cut. Women covered their faces and bodies with tattoos of plants, flowers, and animals.

Both men and women regularly painted their faces and shoulders with dyes derived from plants, minerals, and oils. Some colors and designs were reserved for special occasions. Although red was the most common color of paint, especially for women, men sometimes wore yellow, black, or white.

Like jewelry, a person's hairstyle indicated his or her place in society. Until puberty, girls wore their hair very short in the front and on the sides but very long in the back. In some parts of Powhatan territory, married women wore their hair all one length, cut just below the ears. In other areas, however, they had short bangs and one long braid in back.

Men shaved the hair on the right side of their heads to keep it from getting tangled with their bowstrings. On the left side, they let their hair grow very long—sometimes up to four feet. After combing and greasing their hair with walnut oil to make it sleek, they usually tied it into a knot. The knot was decorated with feathers, or sometimes with deer antlers, shells, or copper *crescents*. The hairstyle of priests was even more unusual. They shaved the right side of their head but allowed one tuft of hair to grow near their right ear.

Parents began training their children at a very young age for their roles in this complicated society. Both mothers and fathers taught boys to hunt. Each morning, a boy's mother would throw moss in the air for him to shoot arrows at, refusing him breakfast until he hit it.

Some time between the ages of 10 and 15, the most promising boys—those who would become priests and councillors—went through an initiation into manhood known as the *Huskenaw*. To begin the ceremony, everyone in the village joined in a morning-long dance and feast in the woods. Dressed in their finest clothes, the Indians danced in circles around a fire. A group of men wearing black horns on their heads and holding green branches stood in the middle. Occasionally during the dance, these men would emit horrible noises, hurl their branches away, and descend upon a small tree and tear it down. They then resumed dancing in the center of the circle.

When everyone was thoroughly exhausted, the boys to be initiated, who were painted white, were brought into the circle. They were ceremonially captured amid much weeping and moaning from the women in the audience. After a great feast, the boys were symbolically killed, and older men danced around their bodies as they lay on the ground. The initiates were then taken into the woods for nine months. They were given a drug, perhaps jimsonweed, which seemed to inspire madness and was supposed to make them forget their previous lives. Having been ritually killed, they were reborn as men and returned to their village. Because they were supposed to remember nothing of their families, it was thought that their loyalty would be only to Okewas and their werowance.

When girls reached puberty, they were considered ready for marriage. Courtship involved a man giving a woman game he had killed, which was supposed to persuade her that he was a good provider. When a woman accepted a marriage proposal, her suitor visited her parents to negotiate a bride-price—the valuable goods he would give her family. After gathering the items he would need to set up a household—a house, pots, bedding—he delivered the bride-price to his fiancée's parents and returned home. The bride then traveled to the groom's new house, where her father joined the couple's hands. The groom's father broke a string of beads over the couple's heads. They were now married.

Marriage brought a man status because it meant that he was mature and capable of providing for others. A man could have more than one wife, but he was expected to be able to support all of them. Thus marriage to more than one woman brought greater status because it indicated greater wealth and hunting ability. Sometimes second and third marriages were meant to be temporary. The couple agreed to stay together for only a year; if they remained together longer, the marriage was expected to be permanent. Both husbands and wives could have affairs, and divorce was also permitted.

Like most aspects of Powhatan culture, the way people were buried depended on their status in society. Ordinary people were wrapped in mats and skins and buried with a

The bodies of dead werowances were preserved and kept in the Powhatans' temples. A model of Okewas watched over the corpses.

few of their possessions. The deceased's female relatives painted their faces black and wailed loudly for a day. In some cases, corpses were placed on a high platform. Every few years, the bones would be taken down and buried together in a large pit.

When a werowance died, his bones were removed from his body, cleaned, and then put back into his skin, which was preserved. The body was put in the village temple along-side the bodies of past werowances. It was believed that only werowances and priests went to the afterlife, a lovely place with plentiful fruits and berries.

In this highly *stratified* society, one man—Powhatan—stood above all others. He was not just a werowance but a *mamanatowick*, or "great king." He had inherited power over eight tribes, and by the end of the 16th century, he had brought another 20 tribes under his control. The werowances of all these tribes paid him tribute. He had many houses and huge fields that were tended by his subjects just for his use. He also had more wives than anyone else—by some accounts more than 100. He kept about a dozen wives at one time. Most of them only stayed with him until bearing a child. After that, they would either return to their villages or be given to a faithful councillor.

When the English colonists arrived in 1607, Powhatan had already gained control over most of the region and was reaching the peak of his power. If the newcomers were going to survive in the Tidewater, they would have to deal with him. ▲

A 19th-century painting
showing the arrival of the
Jamestown colonists in
Powhatan's realm.

Chapter 4

Powhatan's Empire

The first contact between Europeans and Native Americans in the Chesapeake Bay region most likely took place in the 1520s, when Spanish and Portuguese ships arrived in the area. These travelers were just explorers, however, who did not try to build settlements.

But around 1560, the Spanish decided to establish a colony in the area. They kidnapped a young Indian and taught him Spanish so he could serve as an interpreter. They also baptized the young man as a Christian and renamed him Don Luis. In 1570, Don Luis returned to the Tidewater accompanied by a group of *missionaries,* people who want to convert others to their religion. Don Luis soon left the missionaries because he wanted to live among his own people. The Spanish priests pressured him to return to their *mission.* This angered him, and in 1571 he led a war party to the mission, killing all the Spanish except one young boy. Seeking to avenge the death of the priests, the Spanish attacked the next year, killing 30 Indians. This ended the first disastrous interaction between Europeans and Powhatans.

In the 1580s, the English began trying to colonize the area. Their first attempts failed, but in the spring of 1607, three British ships sailed into Chesapeake Bay and up the James River. They stopped at various villages where the Indians greeted them with great hospitality, often serving them lavish feasts. As a display of friendship, the English gave the Indians gifts of glass beads, bells, and needles. At Appamatuck, the newcomers were met by a man holding a bow and arrow in one hand and a tobacco pipe in the other. He was offering them the choice between war and peace. Although the English did not understand his meaning, they nonetheless correctly chose the pipe. The colonists eventually selected a spot for their new settlement, christening the site Jamestown.

Despite the warm welcome afforded them, the English found the Native Americans perplexing. Unable to distinguish between the various Powhatan groups, the settlers were surprised when some proved friendly while others raided the English fort.

Although suspicious of the English, the Powhatans at first did not consider them a threat because the newcomers hardly even seemed capable of taking care of themselves. The site they had chosen for their settlement lacked drinking water and was near a swamp that would soon be swarming with mosquitoes. By summer, many colonists became ill from drinking bad water. They were also running short of food. Many of the settlers came from the upper classes and felt they were above performing manual labor. Others were businessmen who had traveled to the New World in search of quick money. As a result, the colonists were unwilling or unable to plant the necessary crops. For the Powhatans, providing for oneself and one's family was the highest priority. To them, the English seemed utterly inept.

For a few months, Powhatan simply observed the newcomers. He let each of his tribes deal with the settlers as they saw fit. Had he known that the English were not just visiting but intended to stay, he probably would have destroyed the young colony. But

Metal bells and a trade token, which the Jamestown colonists traded to the Powhatans for food and furs.

they seemed harmless, and he liked the idea of trading for their metal goods. He also thought they might be useful allies against enemy tribes.

On June 15, 1607, Powhatan finally contacted the Jamestown settlement. He announced to the English that he wanted peace and informed them that he had ordered his tribes to cease raiding the colony. Throughout the summer, Powhatan sent gifts of food to the English.

The condition of the colony worsened, however. About half of the 100 settlers died during the summer. The expected supply ships failed to arrive from England. By fall, the Indians' corn was ripe, and they sold some of it to the starving colonists. But the crops were not plentiful that year. The neighboring

Indians did not have sufficient supplies to provide the settlers with corn all winter.

John Smith, a member of the colony's governing council, decided to go on trading expeditions to secure corn from tribes that were farther away. He convinced many Indian villages to sell him small portions of their stores. But these Indians also had limited supplies and became less friendly as he kept pestering them for more.

During a December expedition, Smith stumbled across a hunting party led by

This engraving shows Captain John Smith being captured by the Powhatans (top) and a later battle with the Pamunkeys (bottom). Smith's capture in 1607 led to his alleged rescue by Pocahontas.

How they tooke him prisoner in the Oaze 1607.

C. Smith bindeth a saluage to his arm fighteth with the King of Pamaunkee and all his company, and slew 3 of them.

Powhatan's brother Opechancanough and was taken prisoner. Opechancanough took Smith to Werowocomoco, Powhatan's capital city, where Powhatan greeted Smith with great ceremony. During their discussions, Smith told Powhatan of the lands that lay beyond the ocean. When Powhatan asked why the English had come to his territory, Smith lied, saying the English ships had been damaged and forced ashore.

Powhatan told Smith that if the colonists moved from their present settlement to a village closer to him, he would give them food in exchange for metal tools and copper ornaments. He then sent Smith on his way. It was during these conversations, Smith later claimed, that Pocahontas saved him from execution. Although the English did not move their settlement, Powhatan nonetheless kept them well fed, saving the colony from starvation.

But relations between the Powhatans and the English grew worse in the next few years, as the English showed no sign of going home. Each group occasionally conducted raids against the other. Harvests were also bad in these years, causing hardship for both the Indians and the English. Because of their mutual hostility, the Indians were not inclined to sell the colonists corn; they had barely enough to feed themselves. The English, who were better armed, sometimes threatened the Indians, forcing them to surrender their winter food supplies. Powhatan, in turn, tried to take advantage of the settlers' food shortage by demanding guns and swords in exchange for food. Though he was eager to make such trades, he was also more than willing to starve the English out.

By May 1610, the colonists were so desperate that they decided to abandon Jamestown. Powhatan would again have complete control over his empire. But the day after the English set sail for home, they encountered a ship from a fleet bringing supplies and 300 new settlers. With these reinforcements, they turned around and went back to Jamestown.

The new settlers were more hostile toward the Powhatans. They destroyed the Indians' fields and temples and burned entire villages. They demolished the town of Paspahegh, killing every Indian they found, including women and children. This broke the most basic rule of Powhatan warfare. The Powhatans fought back as best they could. Although the English may not have realized it, the Indians now considered themselves at war.

In the next few years, the English con-
quered more Powhatan villages, setting up
new settlements and plantations. Because
the English now had other trading partners
and were growing more food, they were no
longer dependent on the Powhatans' corn.
The Indians engaged in small raids against
English settlements, but these did little to
stop the European expansion.

The situation grew worse, and skirmishes
continued until April 1613, when a colonist
named Samuel Argall kidnapped Pocahontas. She was taken to Jamestown where she
was held hostage for about a year. During
that time, she was trained in the ways of
English culture and became a Christian,
taking the name Rebecca. She also fell in
love with one of her tutors, a man named
John Rolfe.

The couple married in April 1614. Although
Powhatan did not attend the wedding, the
union brought peace between his people
and the colonists. The couple eventually
had one son, Thomas. The family went to
England in 1616, where Pocahontas was
shown off in British society and met the
queen. While preparing to return to Virginia
the following year, Pocahontas fell ill. She
died before she left England.

Meanwhile, too tired to fight, Powhatan left much of the responsibility of ruling to his brothers. He died in April 1618, past the age of 70, ending a reign that had built an empire.

▲

On March 22, 1622,
the Powhatans rose up
against the Jamestown
colonists, killing 330
settlers in a surprise attack.

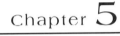

Chapter 5

The Vanishing Tribes

With Powhatan's death, the title of mama-natowick passed to his brother Opichapam. However, Opichapam lacked the vigor and *charisma* to lead an empire. The real ruler was Powhatan's brother Opechancanough, who had grown powerful in the last few years of Powhatan's reign.

But even the more forceful Opechancanough was not able to resist the settlers' expansion when he first assumed power. The last two years of Powhatan's reign had yielded poor harvests, and hunger was widespread. *Epidemics* of smallpox, measles, and influenza also swept through

45

the area. Although these diseases affected both the colonists and the Native Americans, many more Indians than Europeans died from them. Because the diseases had long existed in Europe, the colonists had natural *immunity* to them. But the Powhatans had never been exposed to these diseases before, so their bodies had no resistance to them.

The British presence in the colony was also growing. John Rolfe, Pocahontas's husband, had introduced Brazilian tobacco into Virginia, and it soon became a valuable cash

A drawing of the tobacco plant native to North America (left) and one that Pocahontas's husband John Rolfe imported from Brazil (right). Tobacco farming was a great source of wealth for the English and was largely responsible for the colony's success.

crop. To encourage new settlers, anyone who could pay their way to the New World was given land on which they could grow tobacco. That the land did not belong to the colony did not seem to bother the English. Colonists in search of quick money began arriving in droves. Between 1618 and 1622, the English population in Virginia jumped from 400 to 1,240.

The English also increased their efforts to convert the Powhatans to Christianity. Indian parents were encouraged to send their children to be brought up by British families. In English culture, it was common for children to be sent to boarding schools and thus raised by other people. But this was unheard of among the Powhatans. To them, the idea that someone else was better able to raise their children was insulting. Besides, the Powhatans knew that their children would most likely just be used as a cheap source of labor.

Opechancanough maintained a peaceful and friendly attitude in the face of the colony's expansion and missionary efforts. When an Englishman killed one of his advisers, he did not complain. He had a plan that had been in the works for much too long to ruin casually. Instead, he reaffirmed the truce between the Powhatans and the English. Peace allowed unarmed

Indians to freely enter British settlements to trade and work.

On the morning of Good Friday, March 22, 1622, a large group of Powhatans arrived at various English settlements as they normally would, behaving in a friendly manner. However, at a time set by Opechancanough, the Indians without warning grabbed weapons from the English and attacked them. The English were caught completely off guard. By the day's end, 330 settlers—more than a quarter of the colony's population—were dead.

Because Opechancanough assumed that such a successful assault would drive the English out of Powhatan territory and back to England where they belonged, he did not mount another raid until September. Instead of fleeing, however, the English became determined to destroy the Powhatan tribes.

The English cut down the Indians' crops, smashed their canoes and temples, burned entire villages, and killed any stray Indians they came across. In May 1623, seeking a truce so that both sides could plant crops, Opechancanough met with English leaders. At the end of the peace talks, toasts were made. But the English had poisoned the Indians' drinks. As some Indians became ill and collapsed to the ground and others

continued on page 57

PAMUNKEY POTTERY

For more than 200 years, the Pamunkey Indians have made pottery, pipes, and other objects out of clay. These potters, most of them women, traditionally made dishes, pots, and jars for their own use and also sold some to non-Indians.

After they dug up the clay, potters mixed it with ground-up shells to strengthen it. They then shaped it by hand and rubbed it smooth with a shell or stone. Sometimes they scratched patterns into the pots before placing them in a fire to harden.

Over the years, these handmade objects were slowly replaced by manufactured kitchenware. In the 1930s, however, the Pamunkeys revived the art and began selling pottery to tourists. A pottery school was set up on the Pamunkey reservation by the state of Virginia. There the Pamunkeys could practice their craft and learn non-Indian methods of pottery making. Today, some Pamunkey artists make clay pots on potter's wheels, paint them with glaze, and fire them in kilns. Others, however, still work in the traditional style, keeping alive the ways of their ancestors.

A clay pipe bowl, about 4¼ inches high. This object and those on the next two pages were acquired in 1892–93 from Pamunkey chief Terrill Bradby by ethnologist J. G. Pollard.

A handcrafted cup with 3 legs, measuring 5 inches high and 2½ inches in diameter.

A pipe bowl, about two inches high. The multiple stems allowed five people to smoke it at once.

A two-inch-high pipe bowl. The Pamunkey may have learned to make multi-stemmed pipe bowls from their Catawba Indian neighbors.

A painted oval jar, 5¼ inches high. This and the other objects on these two pages were probably made by students at the Pamunkey pottery school in the 1930s and 1940s.

This Pamunkey jar, painted with a delicate swirling pattern, measures only 3¾ inches high.

A jar, 4½ inches high. The Pamunkey used cords, reeds, pointed sticks, or their fingernails to carve designs into wet clay.

A crosshatch design has been etched into this 3¾-inch jar.

A heavily glazed bowl, about 4½ inches in diameter and painted with white, green, purple, and black pigments. This object and the other two shown here were probably made in the mid-20th century. All are characteristic of the pottery school tradition.

A bowl, 4½ inches in diameter. The designs may have been inspired by those on southwestern tribes' pottery.

A painted 3½-inch vase. Teachers at the pottery school introduced the Pamunkey to pan-Indian designs—patterns used not only by their tribe but by Indians across the country.

A fish-shaped dish, eight inches long and six inches wide, made in the
1930s. Aquatic motifs were popular with Pamunkey potters throughout the
20th century.

continued from page 48

attempted to escape, the English opened fire on them. Although Opechancanough was poisoned, he survived.

War dragged on for another 10 years. Although a decade of peace followed that, it brought little relief to the Powhatans. As disease decimated the Indians' population, the English settlements expanded. By 1640, there were about 8,100 British colonists in Virginia; the Native American population had fallen below 5,000.

The colonists had an insatiable hunger for land on which to grow tobacco. Because tobacco produced quick wealth, they always wanted more and more land. Growing tobacco also used up the nutrients in the soil very quickly, so the same land could not be farmed for very many years in a row. The constant need for wnew farmland led to steady encroachment on the Indians' territory.

On April 18, 1644, Opechancanough made one last attempt to oust the colonists from his territory. His warriors killed 400 settlers in the opening attack, but the British presence was now so large that they easily regrouped and went on the offensive. After two years of devastating English raids, the Powhatans could resist no longer.

In 1646, Opechancanough was captured and taken to Jamestown. Although he was over 80 years old and unable to walk without help, he never acknowledged defeat. He refused to sign a treaty. After being in prison only a short time, he was shot in the back by an English guard.

Necotowance, his successor, did sign a treaty. This treaty conceded that Necotowance was a subject of the king of England. As evidence of the king's rule over his territory, Necotowance agreed to pay a tribute of 20 beaver skins every year to the colonial governor. The treaty gave the English possession of the lowlands between the James and York rivers. The only Powhatans permitted to enter this territory were messengers from Necotowance, and they had to wear striped shirts. Any other Native American who entered this region would be shot on sight.

Necotowance lost power after 1649. From then on, each Powhatan tribe was ruled by its individual werowance. The empire that Powhatan had built had vanished.

To protect their territory from further English expansion, three werowances asked the colonial legislature for grants of land for their tribes. The legislature agreed to allow the tribes to keep for themselves certain pieces of land, known as reservations. But the settlers were greedy for the Indians' fertile lands. Ignoring the boundaries set by law, they moved onto the reservations. Although the Indians complained to the colonial government, they were forced onto smaller and smaller pieces of land.

None of the reservations were large enough to sustain the Powhatans' traditional way of life. The land, though adequate for farming, was not sufficient for hunting and gathering. Under these circumstances, many Indians were forced to work for the English in order to survive.

A few Indians worked in the colony itself as servants. Many of these servants had been captured by the English during wars and had never been released. Their status was very similar to that of the African slaves. Colonists had begun buying slaves in 1619, and their numbers were increasing rapidly.

Indian children were sometimes sent by their parents to work for white families. Although the children were supposed to be released from servitude when they turned 25, they were often not allowed to leave. In many cases, colonists simply kidnapped children, and if questioned, they claimed that the child's parents or werowance had sold the child to them.

Some Powhatan women earned money by selling traditional goods such as baskets, pipes, and pottery, but they had to change the design of these items to suit English tastes. For instance, they made pots with handles and legs to be used for cooking in fireplaces, as was the British custom.

Some Powhatan men were hired as hunters. Because wolves threatened British livestock, the colonists offered the Indians money to kill the animals. But the Powhatans believed that the reason to hunt was to acquire food and skins, not simply to kill. Since they did not eat wolf meat, very few Indians earned money by killing wolves. Other Powhatans worked as guides or built weirs for the English.

Many interactions between the Powhatans and colonists were more strained. Problems frequently arose because settlers let their hogs, which were identified only by a mark on their ear, roam freely through the woods. The Powhatans were used to hunting whatever game they found in the forests, so they sometimes killed English-men's hogs. Once, after apologizing to a colonist whose hogs were killed, a werow-ance also pointed out that the English had killed some of his deer. The colonist claimed there was a difference because the pigs were marked and the deer were not. The werowance replied, "Indeed, none of my deer are marked, and by that you may know them to be mine; and when you meet with any that are marked you may do with them what you please; for they are none of mine."

The 1670s saw great economic unrest among the settlers. High taxes, low tobacco prices, and drought made life difficult for them. Although the colonists were actually angry with their own political leadership, they took out their frustrations on the Indians. After being wrongly attacked and imprisoned, a group of Indians broke out of the fort where they were held. They later raided some plantations in revenge. Using this incident as an excuse, a group of rebellious Englishmen under the leadership of Nathaniel Bacon made war against the Powhatans. This was the last major military confrontation between colonists and Indians in the Tidewater. Bacon's men forced the Pamunkeys out of their village and hunted them down in a nearby swamp. Many of the Indians were killed, and the others were captured and paraded through the streets of Jamestown.

In May 1677, a new treaty was signed that reaffirmed the Powhatans' status as subjects of the British crown. It also established new, smaller reservations for the tribes. But again the settlers paid no attention to the boundaries.

Although contact with the colonists had altered aspects of the Powhatans' traditional

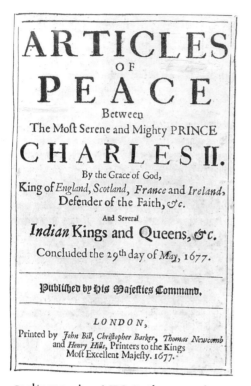

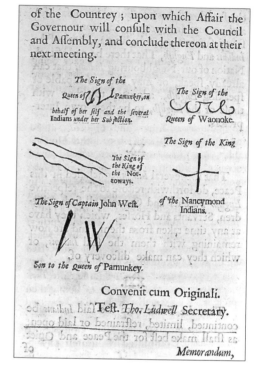

culture, in 1700 that culture was still strong. Most Powhatan men continued to hunt, although they used guns instead of bows and arrows. With guns, they did not need to worry about getting their hair tangled, so they wore it long on both sides. Although their clothing styles remained the same, the clothes were often made from cloth rather than skins. Most Powhatans continued to follow their traditional religion. They still spoke their native language, but most could also speak some English. Despite being surrounded by whites—by this time in Virginia there were 100,000 colonists and less than 1,000 Indi-

The title and signature pages of a 1677 treaty between several Tidewater tribes and the king of England.

ans—the Powhatans fought tenaciously to maintain their culture.

While the number of Indians was dropping, the number of black slaves in the region was booming. To Virginia's whites, race was all-important. A person was defined as either white or nonwhite, and all nonwhites were considered inferior. In 1705, the colony passed a "black code," a series of laws concerning race. Although Indians who lived on reservations had special status, those who lived among whites were classified as non-whites and were subject to the same restrictions as free blacks and mulattoes (people with mixed black and white ancestry). This meant that nonreservation Indians could not hold public office or serve as witnesses in court. Whites could not marry nonwhites, and any white woman who had a child by a nonwhite could be fined and made a servant. Any child with only one Indian parent—regardless of whether the other parent was black or white—was classified as a mulatto and not an Indian. Because of such laws, those Indians who had skin light enough to pass as white usually did so. Facing such discrimination, they had little reason to want to be considered Indians.

Indians on reservations fared little better than those living among whites. The Nansatico tribe complained to colonial authorities about whites settling on their territory. When the authorities did nothing, some Nansatico warriors took matters into their own hands by killing a white family. The colonial authorities arrested all 49 members of the tribe. Five men were found guilty and hanged. Despite being found not guilty, the rest were deported to the West Indies. With a single stroke, an entire tribe was wiped out.

Meanwhile, other reservations shrank, and Indian populations dwindled. Tribes merged or *disintegrated.* Some Indians *assimilated* into white society; others joined free black communities. By the end of the 18th century, only the Pamunkeys and the Accomacs still had reservations and were officially recognized as Indians.

As a result, much of Powhatan culture was lost. By 1800, most Powhatans had become Christians. Their language was virtually extinct, a situation noted in 1787 by future U.S. president Thomas Jefferson in his book *Notes on the State of Virginia.* He wrote, "The Pamunkies are reduced to about 10 or 12 men. . . . The older ones among them preserve their language in a small degree, which are the last vestiges on earth, as far as we know, of the Powhatan language."

Although the Powhatan language disappeared, some of its words remain in use. Many cities and rivers in Virginia still bear Powhatan names. *Moccasin, tomahawk, raccoon,* and *opossum* are all words that the Powhatan language contributed to English.

During the early 19th century, southern whites' racial attitudes hardened. As they became more worried about the work of northern abolitionists—people who wanted to end the institution of slavery—and the possibility of slave revolts, they enacted stricter laws governing the activities of free nonwhites. Nonwhites had to carry certificates proving that they were free. Without these certificates, they could be jailed. If no one testified to their freedom, they could be sold into slavery. It became illegal for nonwhites to lead meetings and have guns. They also lost the right to jury trials; instead, justices decided their fates, just as they did with slaves.

Such laws made it necessary for Powhatans to be able to prove their "Indianness." Although reservation Indians remained exempt from some of these laws, their status was constantly threatened. As the Civil War approached, only the Pamunkeys still had official recognition. To survive, they would have to struggle to maintain their identity as Indians. ▲

A 1918 photograph of George Major Cook, chief of the Pamunkey Indians. By the end of the 19th century, many Indian men wore their hair long to proclaim their Indian identity.

Chapter 6

Struggle for Survival

The conclusion of the Civil War in 1865 put an end to slavery in the United States. All blacks in the South were freed. In Virginia, the war's end also brought new definitions of "colored person" and "Indian." An 1866 law stated, "Every person having one-fourth or more of negro blood shall be deemed a colored person, and every person not a colored person having one-fourth or more of Indian blood shall be deemed an Indian." Thus, to be legally considered an Indian, a person had to be at least one-fourth Native American but less than one-fourth black.

After the war's end, whites retained their dominance in southern society. Most whites still believed they were naturally superior to blacks. Laws were passed keeping the races separated in public spaces, a concept called segregation. Blacks were not allowed to ride in train cars, attend schools, eat in restaurants, use bathrooms or water fountains, or live in houses that were reserved for whites. The facilities for blacks were far inferior to those for whites.

Because of such laws, the Powhatans fought hard to keep their Indian status. If they were considered colored instead of Indian, they would be treated as badly as blacks. For instance, only reservation Indians could ride in the railroad cars reserved for whites. Those who lived off reservations suffered the indignity of riding in the "colored" car. So the Powhatans began forming their own institutions to proclaim their Indian identity. In 1865, they established their own church, the Pamunkey Indian Baptist Church.

They demanded separate schools from blacks for their children, who were not allowed in white schools. This antagonized whites who did not want to pay for another set of schools. But it also angered blacks. They thought that, since they were both oppressed by whites, the Indians should be their allies rather than try to separate themselves.

The schools for Native Americans offered limited curriculums. The only one that taught anything about Native American culture was a pottery school established on the Pamunkey reservation in 1932. But even there, a white teacher taught the students to use a pottery wheel instead of teaching them to make pottery in the traditional way. The teacher also showed the students how to make designs he thought were typically "Indian" but which actually had nothing to do with their culture.

Because of the discrimination they suffered if they were considered colored, many Powhatans tried to make themselves more easily identifiable as Indians. This was not easy because their traditional way of life was almost completely gone, and they were now living like white people. Even the Pamunkeys had to constantly prove that they were really Indians. They sometimes dressed in Indian fashion at public events. But the way the Powhatans had traditionally dressed—wearing virtually nothing—would not have been acceptable in 19th-century Virginia. So instead they wore outfits based on the clothing of other tribes—large headdresses and suede pants, shirts, and dresses that were decorated with fringes and beads.

Because there were so few Indians in Virginia, the Powhatans tried to find other Native Americans to marry. According to the racial purity laws, if they married non-Indians their children would not legally be considered Indian. To find spouses, the Pamunkeys advertised in newspapers from North Carolina to Oklahoma. But Virginia was known as a harsh place for nonwhites, so they had little success.

Although the Pamunkeys had long been the only tribe recognized by Virginia, the Powhatans' pride and the value of legal

Chickahominy leaders pay their tribe's annual tribute to the governor of Virginia in 1919.

Indian status led other tribes to organize. The Pamunkey reservation had been divided into two pieces in the 18th century. In 1894, those living in the part along the Mattaponi River split into a separate tribe called the Mattaponis. In 1901, Indians living off reservations organized a tribe called the Chickahominys. Another group, the Eastern Chickahominys, split off in 1925. Two other tribes, the Upper Mattaponis and the Rappahannocks, organized in the 1920s. But even then, only the Pamunkeys and the Mattaponis had reservations and were recognized by the state.

As the Powhatan tribes organized, Virginia made its racial definitions stricter. In 1924, Virginia turned the "one-drop rule" into law. This rule stated that no one could be called white who had one drop of blood from any other race. The only exceptions were people who were less than $\frac{1}{16}$ Native American: they could still be considered white. This loophole was made for the benefit of the many ruling class whites in Virginia who claimed to be descended from Pocahontas and John Rolfe. The one-drop rule would have forced them to be considered colored, so an exception was made for their sake.

The new law said that nonreservation Indians had to be at least $\frac{1}{4}$ Native American and could not have one drop of black blood. Indians on reservations were still considered Indians only if they were less than $\frac{1}{16}$ black.

Walter Plecker, the head of Virginia's Bureau of Vital Statistics, cruelly enforced this law. He forced the Powhatans to prove they had no black ancestry. But Indian birth certificates and other records, particularly for those living off reservations, were not kept systematically, and many of Virginia's records had been destroyed during the Civil War. Proving Indian heritage was virtually impossible.

Plecker threatened all Powhatans by trying to prove that none of them were Indians. He studied records dating back to 1830. Although the word "colored" was not used in the same way at that time, he assumed it was. If the word was used in an old document, he designated the persons' descendants as colored. He also tried to force county clerks to identify newborn Indian babies as colored. Some bowed to his pressure; others did not. In 1924, he went so far as to say that there were no Indians in Virginia who did not have some black ancestry. To him, this meant that there were no Indians in Virginia.

Plecker's harassment had far-reaching consequences for the Powhatans. Indian children were ejected from white schools,

In the 20th century, several Tidewater tribes have won official recognition from the state of Virginia.

and Plecker threatened a Chickahominy midwife with criminal prosecution, claiming she had falsified records when she wrote "Indian" on a birth certificate. The pressure against the Powhatans was so intense that some moved to northeastern states, where there was less discrimination and people were unlikely to question their heritage. The Powhatans struggled against Plecker's policies until 1946, when he finally retired.

Beginning in the 1950s, the civil rights movement slowly eroded segregation in America. Indians as well as blacks benefited from the civil rights movement. It enabled Powhatans to hold government positions in Virginia for the first time. In the 1970s in Charles City County, a Chickahominy was hired as a county administrator; two Indians held positions on the county planning commission; and another Chickahominy served on the county school board. Other Powhatans have become teachers, doctors, lawyers, and accountants.

A funeral procession by members of the Mattaponi tribe honoring Chief Jacob Vincent Custalow, also known as Thundercloud, in 1982.

The Indian rights movement, which began in the 1960s, increased the Powhatans' visibility and pride. All across the United States, Native Americans joined together to fight for their rights. The movement helped the Pamunkeys mount a lawsuit against the Southern Railway Company. In 1855, the railroad took 22 acres of the Pamunkey reservation to lay a track. The company paid the tribe nothing for the land. In 1971, the Pamunkeys accepted an out-of-court settlement of $100,000, future rent on the land, and the return of seven acres that were not being used by the railroad.

In the past two decades, the Powhatan tribes have thrived. In addition to the Pamunkeys and the Mattaponis, Virginia now also formally recognizes the Eastern and Western Chickahominys, the Upper Mattaponis, the Rappahannocks, and the Nansemonds. This represents great progress compared to 100 years ago, when the state recognized only the Pamunkeys.

Nearly 400 years after the arrival of British colonists in North America, the descendants of the Powhatans have endured. They have outlived early efforts to slaughter them and later efforts to claim they simply did not exist. Above all, they have never forgotten who they are and have remained proud and visible as Native Americans. ▲

GLOSSARY

abduct kidnap

assimilate become a member of a different group of people and adopt their way of life

charisma the ability of a leader to inspire love and loyalty in others

colonial having to do with a settlement or colony ruled by a distant country

crescent a narrow, curved moon shape

disintegrate break apart

epidemic a serious outbreak of disease that strikes a large group of people

immunity the body's natural ability to fight off disease

loincloth a simple garment hanging from the waist

mission a settlement of people attempting to spread their religion in a foreign land

missionary a person who travels to a foreign land to convert the native population to Christianity

puberty the age at which a child's body changes to that of an adult

sapling a small tree

scaffold an open framework

sinew tough fibers that connect muscles to other parts of the body

stratified divided into separate classes

tan make leather from animal skins by treating them with tree bark or materials rich in tannin

tribute gifts or payments to a ruler

vengeful intent on inflicting punishment or revenge

CHRONOLOGY

1520s   First contact between Europeans and Native Americans in the Chesapeake Bay region occurs

1560   Spanish establish colony in the area

late 16th century   Powhatan inherits power over eight tribes and brings another 20 tribes under his control

1607   British colonists found Jamestown, the first permanent English settlement in North America

ca. 1608   Pocahontas allegedly saves Captain John Smith, one of the settlement's leaders

1613   Samuel Argall kidnaps Pocahontas, and she is converted to Christianity

1614   Pocahontas marries John Rolfe

1622   Opechancanough leads an attack on English settlers; 330 are killed

1677   Treaty is signed that reaffirms the Powhatans' status as subjects of the British crown

1705   The colony passes a "black code," a series of racial laws

1790   The Pamunkeys and Accomacs are the only tribes that have reservations and are recognized as Indians

1855   The Southern Railway Company takes 22 acres of the Pamunkey reservation to lay a track

1865   Indians establish their own church, the Pamunkey Indian Baptist Church

1971   The Pamunkeys accept an out-of-court settlement from the Southern Railway Company for $100,000, the return of seven acres, and future rent on the remaining land.

INDEX

ABOUT THE AUTHOR

MELISSA MCDANIEL is a freelance writer and editor living in New York City. Her other books for children include *The Sac and Fox Indians* and a young adult biography of Stephen Hawking.

PICTURE CREDITS

Daily Press, Inc., Newport News, VA: p. 74; The Denver Art Museum: pp. 52, 53, 56; Department of Anthropology, Smithsonian Institution: pp. 49, 50, 51, 54, 55; Jamestown-Yorktown Foundation: p. 14; Library of Congress: pp. 2, 8, 12, 17, 22, 27, 32, 34, 39, 45, 46; National Museum of the American Indian, Smithsonian Institution: p. 66; National Park Service, Colonial National Historic Park: p. 38; New York Public Library, Astor, Lenox, and Tilden Foundations: p. 62; Smithsonian Institution: p. 70.

Maps by Gary Tong: pp. 6, 73.